UNIT 5

Around Our Town

Grade 1

Program Authors

Carl Bereiter, Ph.D.
Andrew Biemiller, Ph.D.
Joe Campione, Ph.D.
Doug Fuchs, Ph.D.
Lynn Fuchs, Ph.D.

Steve Graham, Ph.D.
Karen Harris, Ph.D.
Jan Hirshberg, Ed.D.
Anne McKeough, Ph.D.
Marsha Roit, Ed.D.

Marlene Scardamalia, Ph.D.
Marcy Stein, Ph.D.
Gerald H. Treadway Jr, Ph.D.

Photo Credits

4 Alyssa Jon Hillson Renkas, tuja66/iStock/Getty Images Plus, hxdbzxy/iStock/Getty Images Plus; **5** ©Andersen Ross/Blend Images LLC, Kali Nine LLC/E+/Getty Images, Corbis Super RF/Alamy, NikkosDaskalakis/iStock/Getty Images Plus, Fuse/Getty Images, Glowimages/Getty Images, Henryk T. Kaiser/Photolibrary/Getty Images; **6** Jupiterimages/Getty Images; **7** Steve Geer/Getty Images; **8** Alyssa Jon Hillson Renkas, Thinkstock/Jupiter Images; **9** Ingram Publishing; **10** Bilderbox/INSADCO Photography/Alamy; **11** Hero Images/Getty Images; **12** William Andrew/Getty Images; **13** Steve Geer/Getty Images; **14** Adam Lubroth/Digital Vision/Getty Images; **15** Kroekchai/Getty Images; **16** Betty Wiley/Getty Images; **17** asiseeit/E+/Getty Images; **21** Ariel Skelley/Blend Images; **23** Pixtal/age fotostock, Joe Ferrer/Getty Images; **24** MBI/Alamy; **25** DreamPictures/Blend Images LLC; **26** Izf/iStock/Getty Images, DenisTangneyJr/Getty Images; **30** Photography by Mijang Ka/Getty Images; **32** Blend Images/Alamy; **34** Jupiterimages/Stockbyte/Getty Images; **36** enfi/Getty Images; **40-41** Design Pics/Corey Hochachka; **42** Steve Debenport/iStock/Getty Images; **43** kristian sekulic/Getty Images, Randy Allbritton/Getty Images. **Back Cover:** ©Andersen Ross/Blend Images LLC, Kali Nine LLC/E+/Getty Images, Corbis Super RF/Alamy.

Acknowledgment

Grateful acknowledgment is given to the following publishers and copyright owners for permissions granted to reprint selections from their publications. All possible care has been taken to trace ownership and secure permission for each selection included. In case of any errors or omissions, the Publisher will be pleased to make suitable acknowledgments in future editions.

"Wake Up!" by Eva Grant. From POETRY PLACE ANTHOLOGY. Copyright ©1983 by Edgell Communications, Inc. Reprinted by permission of Scholastic Inc.

MHEonline.com

Copyright © 2016 McGraw-Hill Education

All rights reserved. No part of this publication may be reproduced or distributed in any form or by any means, or stored in a database or retrieval system, without the prior written consent of McGraw-Hill Education, including, but not limited to, network storage or transmission, or broadcast for distance learning.

Send all inquiries to:
McGraw-Hill Education
8787 Orion Place
Columbus, OH 43240

ISBN: 978-0-02-142363-7
MHID: 0-02-142363-6

Printed in the United States of America.

6 7 8 9 MER 26 25 24 23

UNIT 5
Around Our Town

Table of Contents

Unit Overview 4

City Life and Town Life 6
  by Jeri Johnson

Wake Up! 18
  by Eva Grant
  illustrated by Cornelius Van Wright

Places in Our Community 20
  by Nicole DeSalle
  illustrated by Jason Dove

Glossary 42

UNIT 5
Around Our Town

BIG Idea

What places make up a community?

Theme Connections

What places are these people visiting in their community?

 **Background Builder Video**
connected.mcgraw-hill.com

Essential Questions How is living in a city different from living in a small town? How is it the same?

City Life and Town Life

by Jeri Johnson

A community is a group of people in a particular place. Your neighborhood is a community. It is made up of people who live and work there. Homes and schools are part of a community. So are shops and other buildings.

Shops are part of a community.

Cities and towns are two types of communities. In some ways cities and towns are alike. In other ways, they are different. Let's compare a city and a town in the state of New York. Look at New York City and Alden, for example.

Size

New York City is one of the largest cities in the United States. Millions of people live there! Some people live in houses or small apartment buildings. Others live in very tall buildings. People in New York City live close together. They have many neighbors.

These neighbors live in the same building.

Alden is a town in New York state. It is much smaller than New York City. About ten thousand people live in Alden. It has fewer buildings and a lot of open land. Homes have larger yards, and buildings have more space between them in Alden than in New York City.

This home has a big yard and no neighbors in sight.

Neighborhoods

New York City is made up of different neighborhoods. Chinatown is one neighborhood. Others are Harlem and Little Italy. Each neighborhood has different types of stores and restaurants. The sidewalks and streets often fill up with people.

Shops in Chinatown sell Chinese gifts and food.

Alden is a rural community. This means it is in the country. It has fewer places for people to visit than New York City. Alden has 20 stores and 14 restaurants. In Alden, the farmers market is a fun place to gather.

Fruits, vegetables, and flowers are for sale at a farmers market.

Services

Because **New York City** has many people, it provides a lot of services. The city has over 1,800 schools. There are about 90 public libraries and 220 fire stations. People enjoy spending time at more than 1,700 city parks and playgrounds.

Thousands of people visit Central Park each day.

Alden provides services for its citizens as well, but it has fewer facilities. It has one library and one fire station. There are four public schools in Alden. It has two town parks and a recreation center.

Firefighters work at a fire station to help keep citizens safe.

Transportation

People in **New York City** often walk from place to place. To get to places that are too far to walk, people use buses or the subway. The city runs the rail and bus systems. Many people also ride on bikes or in taxis.

The subway is a busy place! This train is filled with passengers.

Alden does not have a subway or a city bus system. Most people use cars to drive from place to place. Some commute to a nearby city to work. The roads in Alden are not as crowded as the streets in New York City.

This quiet road leads to a small town.

Watching a fireworks show over New York City is an exciting event!

Some people enjoy living in a big, busy city. New York City is a place with lots of activity! Some people prefer a smaller, quieter setting. Alden is a town where life is less hectic.

These children enjoy watching a parade in their town.

New York City and Alden are different in many ways. But they have one important thing in common. People in both places share good times together!

Essential Question How are mornings different in the city than in the country?

Wake Up!

by Eva Grant
illustrated by Cornelius Van Wright

In the country
Everyone knows
It's morning when
The rooster crows.

But the city's
A different matter!
You're sure to hear
Garbage cans clatter,
Taxis toot,
Buses roar,
A paper slap
Against your door.

In country or city,
Morning sounds say,
"Wake up! Here comes
Another day."

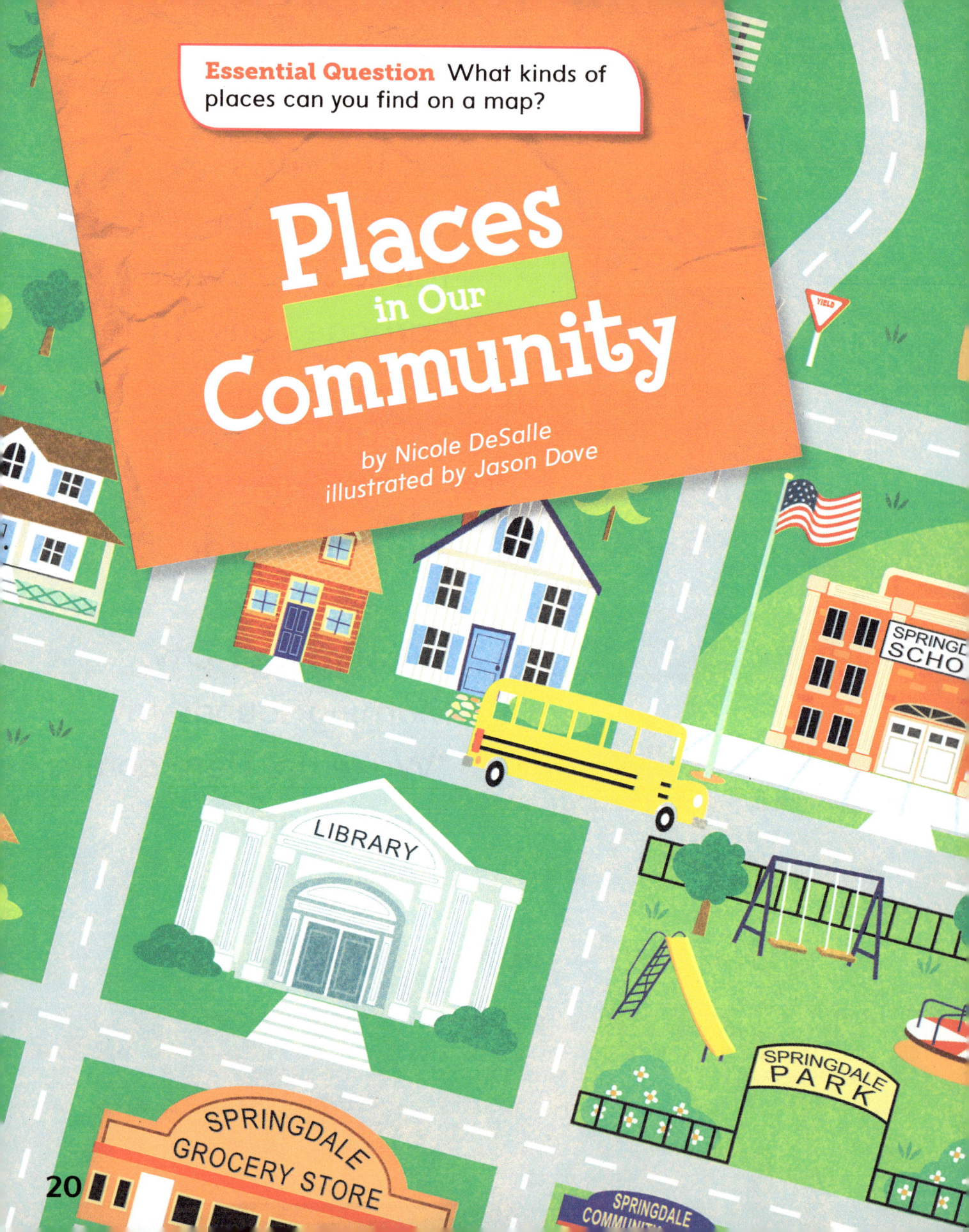

Essential Question What kinds of places can you find on a map?

Places in Our Community

by Nicole DeSalle
illustrated by Jason Dove

Map of Springdale

This community has a school. It is in a town called Springdale. Children come to this school to learn. They learn new things from their teachers and each other every day.

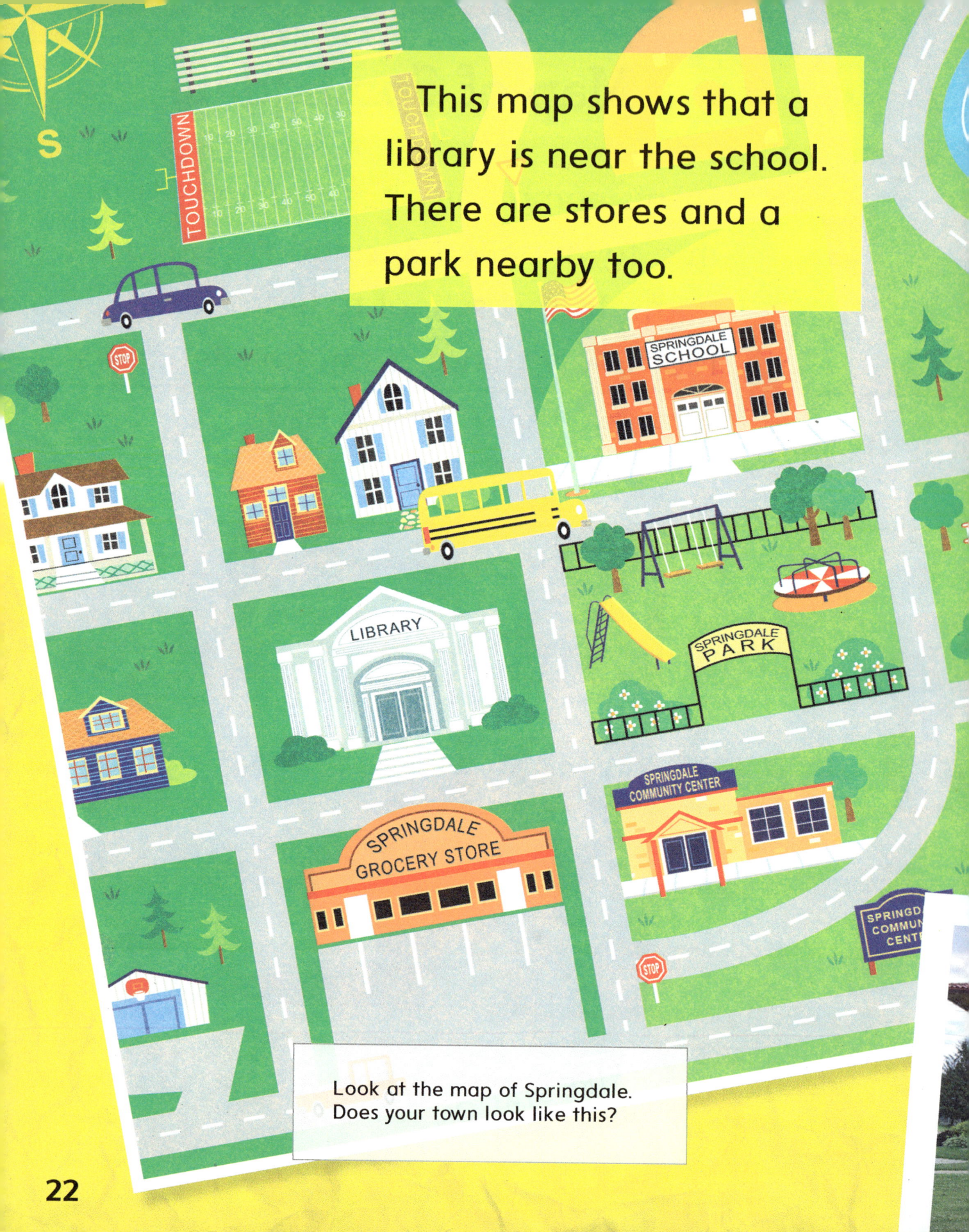

This map shows that a library is near the school. There are stores and a park nearby too.

Look at the map of Springdale. Does your town look like this?

This community has a public library. People come here to find books. They decide which books they would like to borrow and then take them home.

Springdale has a grocery store. People come here to buy things they need. They buy food and beverages at the store. They also buy clothes or things for their homes.

This community also has a fire station. People come here to see the firefighters and their trucks. Firefighters ride the trucks to an emergency. They put out fires and save people who are in trouble.

The community of Springdale is near Stamford in Connecticut.

Stamford is a small city. Downtown Stamford is lively and full of activity. People work in tall buildings. Trains run every day.

Map of Connecticut

Look at the map of Connecticut. Is Stamford near Norwalk? Is it close to Hartford?

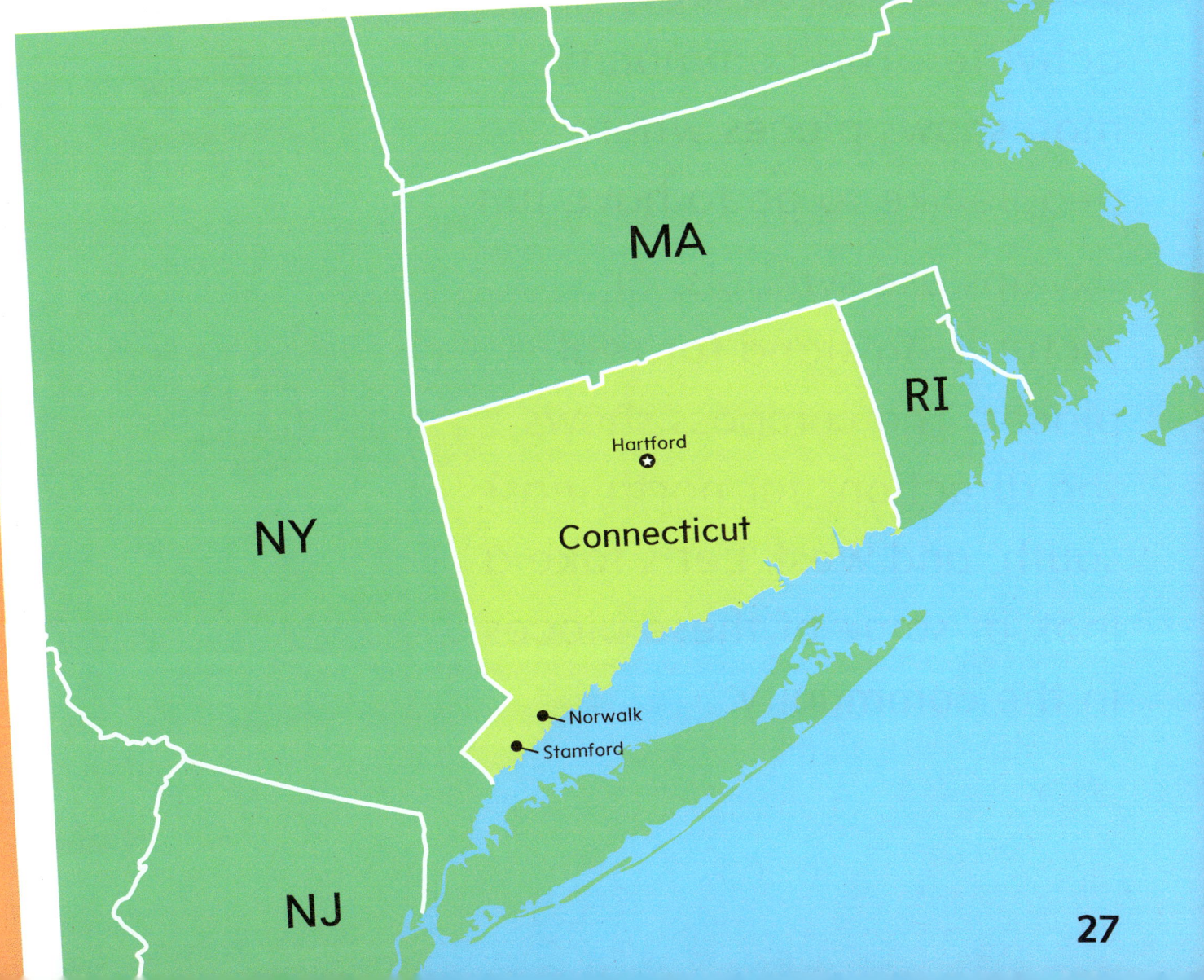

Reading a Map

Towns and cities like Springdale and Stamford have lots of places where people can go to enjoy activities. This community map shows places where people like to go to have fun.

Maps use symbols, or pictures, to stand for real places. The compass shows the directions for north, east, south, and west. Let's take a look at some of these places in the community.

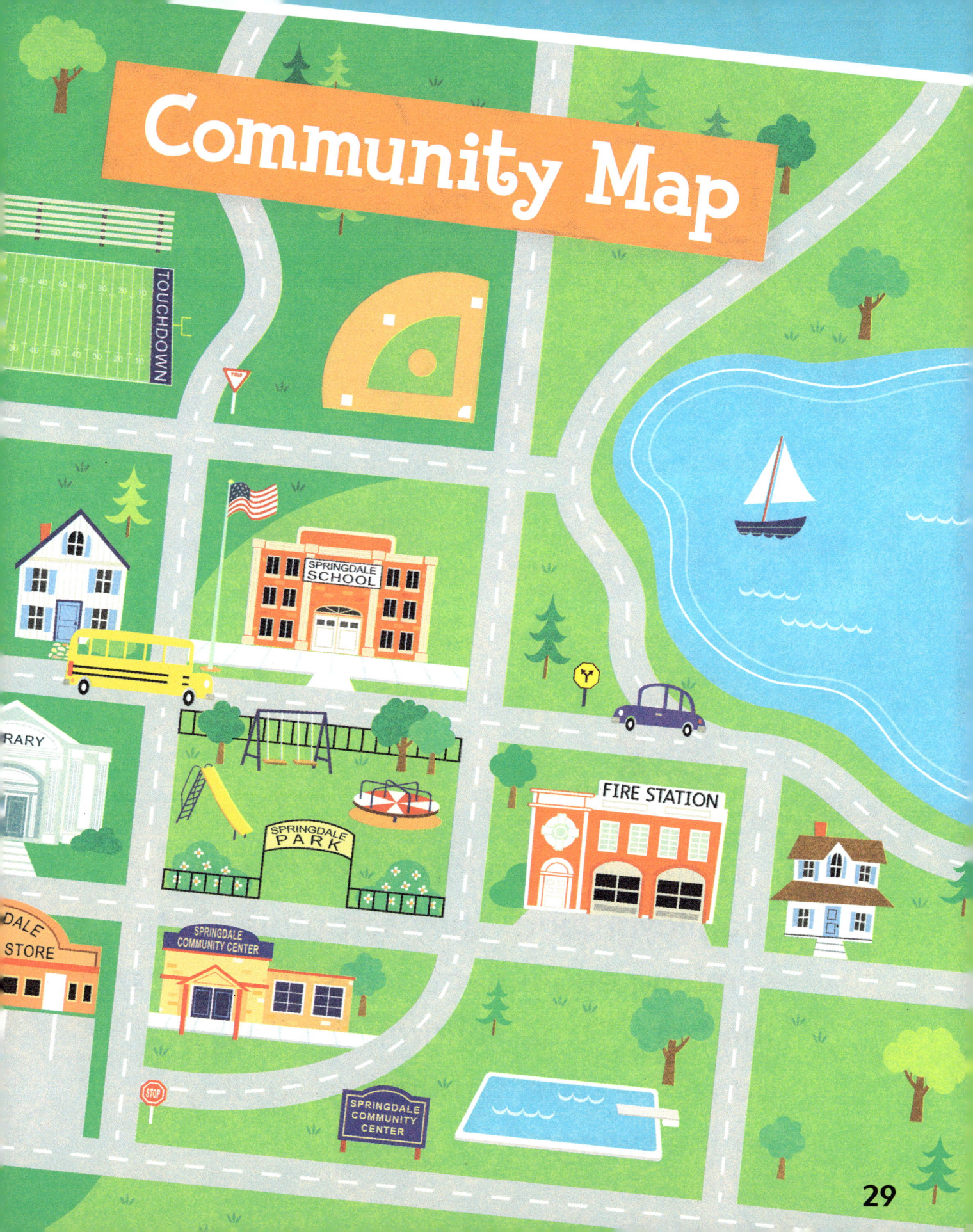

Park

In the park, children like to play on the playground. They scramble up the climbing equipment and swing across the bars. Some children like to go down the slide. Others like to play on the swings.

Neighbors talk to each other as their children play. Some people like to sit on park benches and read books. The park is where everyone can relax and enjoy the fresh air.

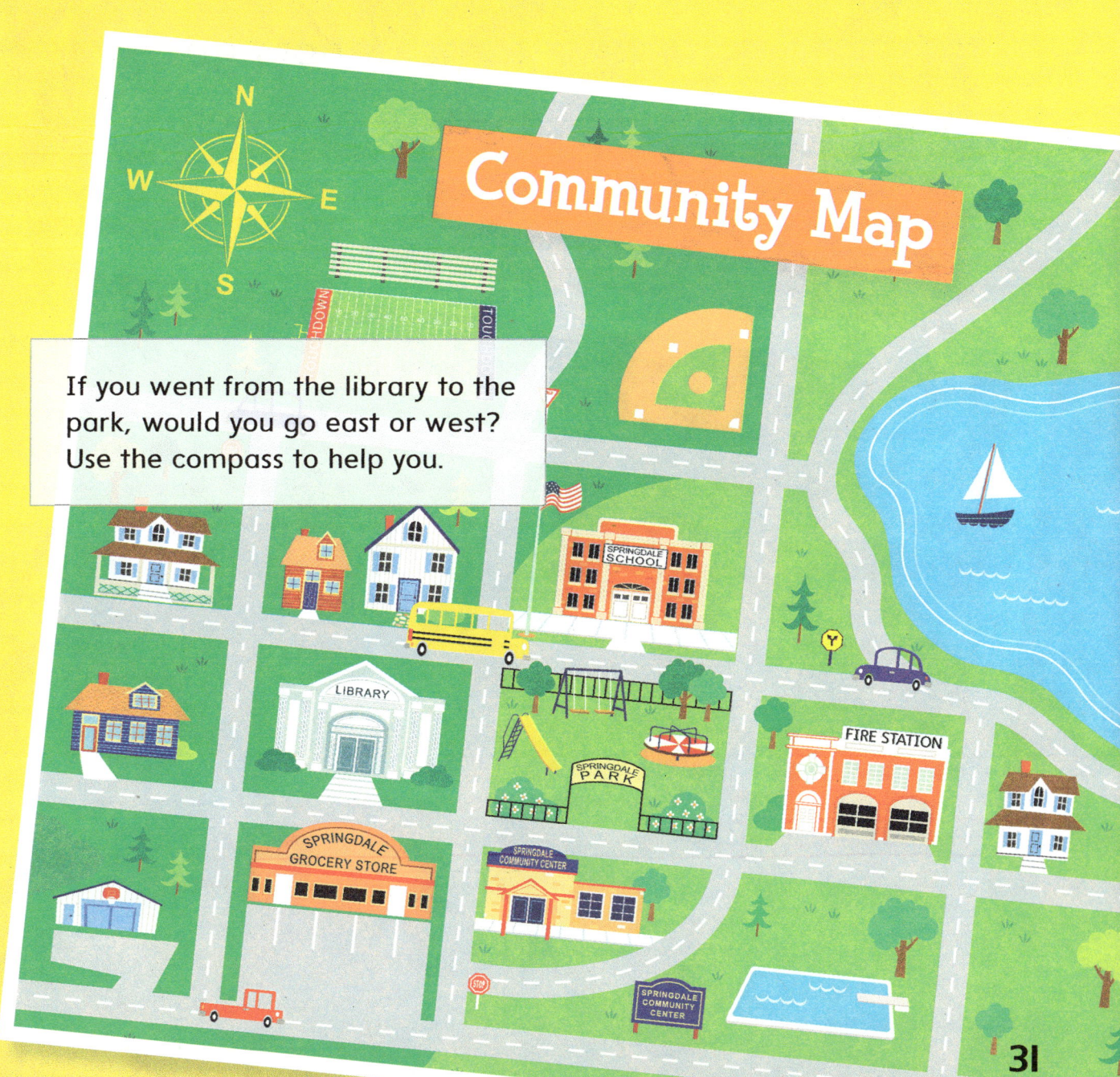

If you went from the library to the park, would you go east or west? Use the compass to help you.

Playing Field

Many communities have fields set up specifically for sports. Teams go there to practice or to play games against other teams. Sometimes neighbors go just to run or to play a game of catch.

If you left the park and went to the playing fields to watch a game, in which direction would you go? Use the compass to help you.

Some people like to watch school sports teams play. Sometimes bands play. Other classmates might do a dance and a cheer.

Community Pool

When the first day of warm weather arrives, people visit the community pool. They visit with friends. Some girls and boys learn how to swim. Others like to play games in the water.

Some people like to relax in the shade and talk. Pool visitors may even bring a picnic lunch! Lifeguards make sure that everyone is safe in the community pool.

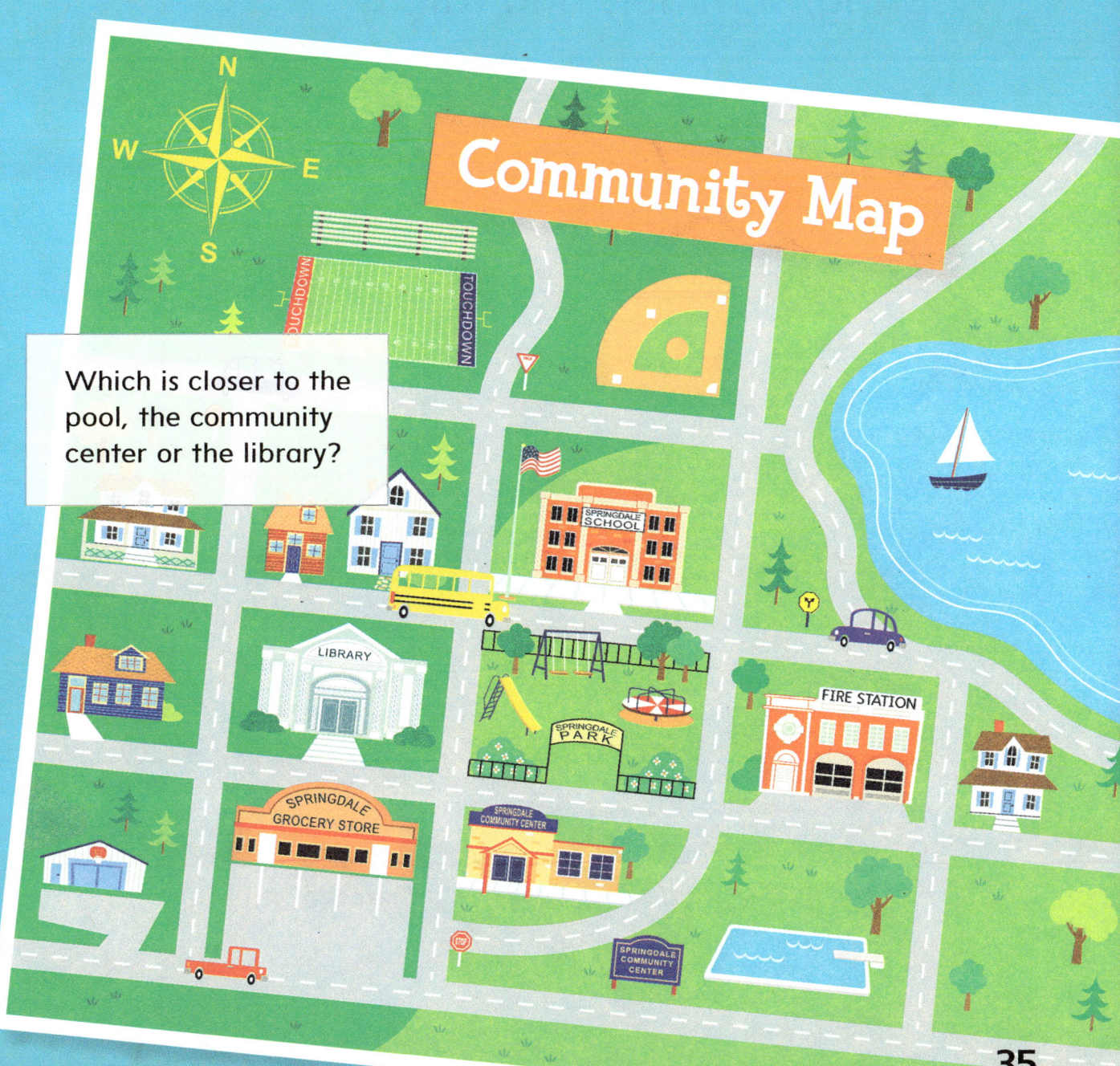

Which is closer to the pool, the community center or the library?

The community of Stamford is in Connecticut, which is a small state in an area called the East Coast. This area has four seasons: winter, spring, summer, and fall.

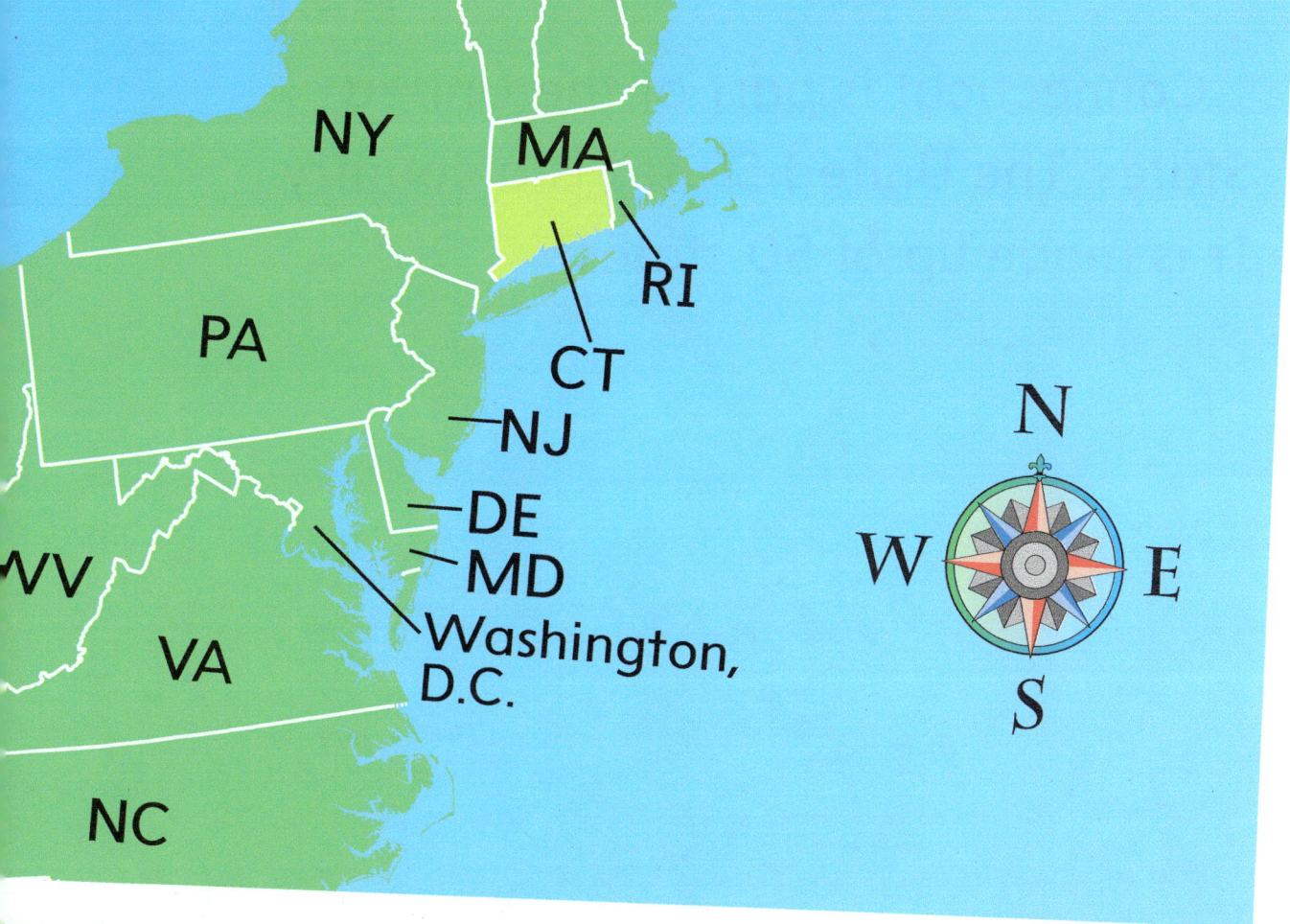

Map of East Coast

Look at the map. New York is west of Connecticut. Rhode Island is on the east side.

What other state borders Connecticut?

Map of the United States

Connecticut is part of the United States. The United States is a country. It is made up of 50 states.

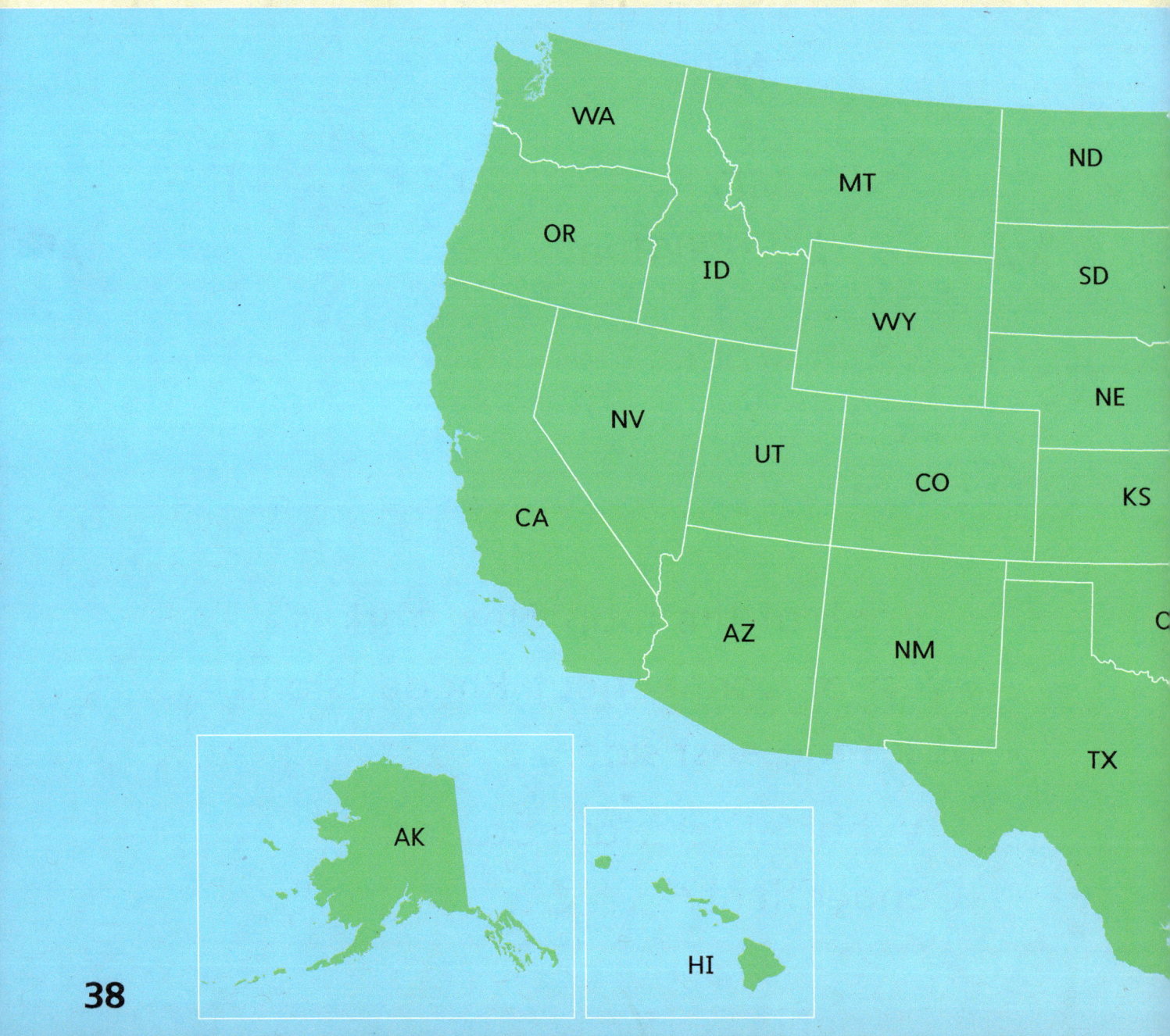

Look at the map. In which state do you live?

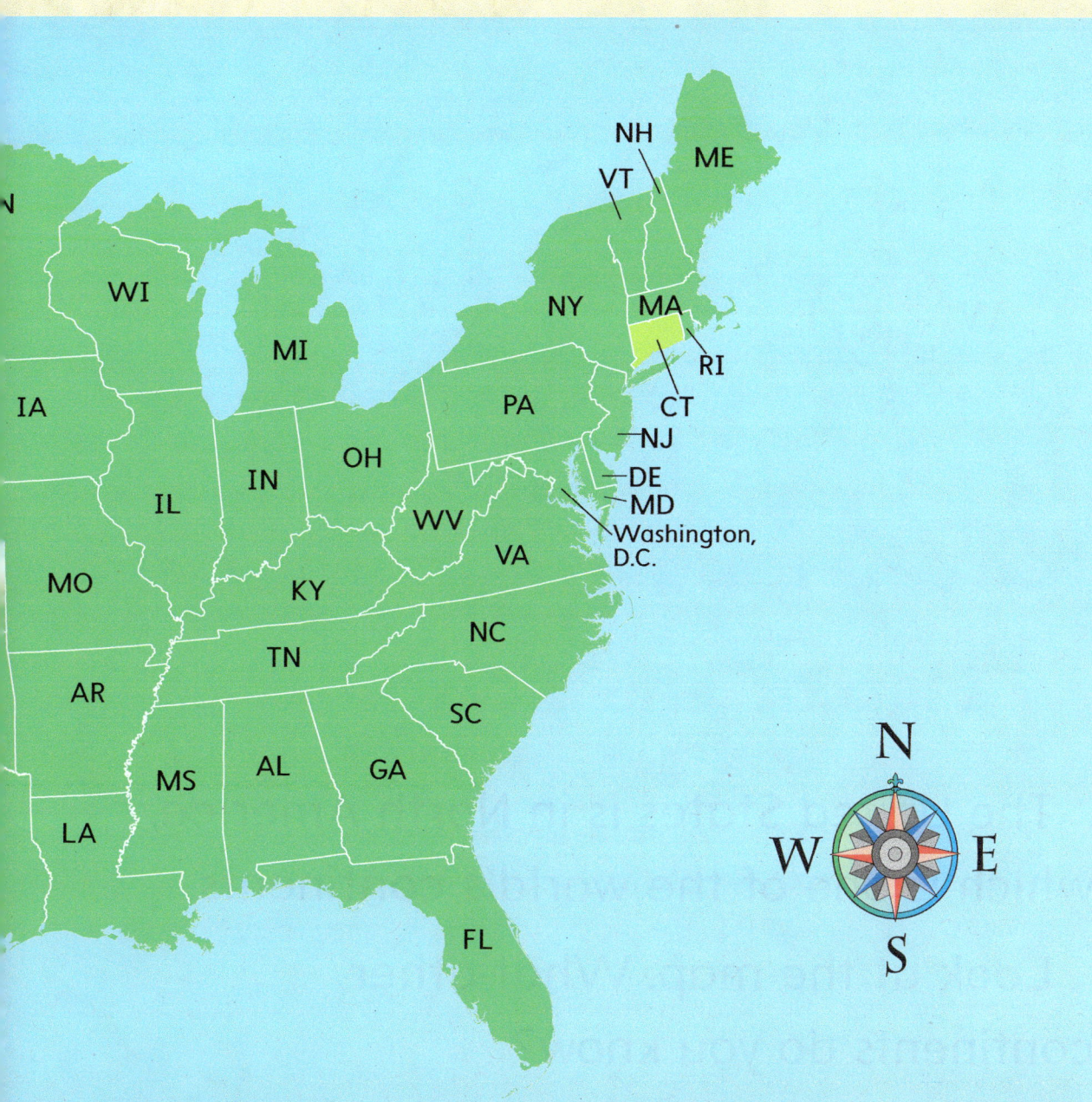

Map of the World

The United States is in North America, which is one of the world's continents.

Look at the map. What other continents do you know?

There are different communities all over the world. What is your community like?

Glossary

B

borders
to be next to

borrow
to take something that belongs to someone else for a period of time before returning it

C

citizens
plural form of **citizen**: a person who lives in a specific place and has rights in that area

common (in common)
something shared by multiple people or things

commute
to travel to and from where you live and where you work

compass
a device that shows direction

F

facilities
plural form of **facility**: a building built for a specific purpose

fewer
a smaller number of

H

hectic
very busy; lots of activity

P

practice
to do something over again and again to become better at it

R

recreation
activities that people enjoy

S

symbols
plural form of **symbol**: a picture or letter that is used to mean something else

T

types
plural form of **type**: a particular group or kind